◀ Star and Stripes

▲ Blue Pinwheels

◀ Another Trip Around the World

▲ Ribbons and Ribbons

How to Make a Quilt in a Hurry

Choosing the Fabric

Old time quilts were traditionally made of 100% cotton, and this is still the fabric that experienced quilters prefer.

Cotton has a number of properties that makes it especially suitable for patchwork. You will find less distortion with cotton fabric which means that your carefully cut small pieces will fit together more easily. If you make a mistake and find a puckered area, a quilt made of 100% cotton often can be ironed flat with a steam iron. In addition, the needle moves through cotton with ease as opposed to some synthetics. If you are hand quilting, this is an extremely valuable quality.

For years, I have always insisted upon pre-washing of all fabrics before using any fabric in a quilt. (Putting yards and yards of fabric into your washing machine and then ironing it before starting to cut certainly is not a way to make a Quilt in a Hurry.) Now I have come almost full circle in my belief that pre-washing fabric is not necessary.

It is necessary to *test* your fabric to make certain that the fabric is colorfast and preshrunk (don't trust those manufacturer's labels). Start by cutting a 2"-wide strip, cut crosswise, of each of the fabrics that you have selected for your quilt. To determine whether the fabric is colorfast, put each strip separately into a clean bowl of extremely hot water, or hold the fabric strip under hot running water. If your fabric bleeds a great deal, all is not necessarily lost. It might only be necessary to wash all of the fabric until all of the excess dye has washed out. Fabrics which continue to bleed after they have been washed several times should be eliminated.

To test for shrinkage, take each saturated strip and iron it dry with a hot iron. When the strip is completely dry, measure and compare it to your original measurements. The fabric industry allows about 2% shrinkage in cotton fabrics. That means that your 45" crosswise fabric should not lose more than 1". If all of your fabric strips shrink about the same amount, then you really have no problem. When you wash your finished quilt, you may achieve the puckered look of an antique quilt. If you do not want this look, you will have to wash and dry all of the fabric before beginning so that shrinkage is no longer a problem. If only one of your fabrics is shrinking more than the others, it will have to be washed and dried, or discarded.

A word about sun fading: I live in an area of intense sunlight. No matter how I try, fabrics fade in my house. Before I make any quilts, I test my fabrics for sun fading. I put samples of my fabric in the window of the room I am intending for my quilt, or—if I'm uncertain—in my sunniest window. After a few days of very strong sunlight, I compare fabrics. If there are changes in color I either discard the fabric, or decide I'm going to like the color as it changes.

Make sure that your fabric is absolutely square. If it is not you will have difficulty cutting your strips. Fabric is woven with crosswise and lengthwise threads. Lengthwise threads should be parallel to the selvage (that's the finished edge along the sides; sometimes the fabric company prints its name along the selvage) and crosswise threads should be perpendicular to the selvage (**Fig 1**). If fabric is off-grain, you can straighten it. Pull gently on the true bias in the opposite direction to the off-grain edge (**Fig 2**). Continue doing this until crosswise threads are at a right angle to lengthwise threads.

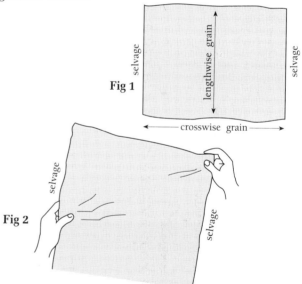

Cutting the Strips

Most of the quilts in this book are made by cutting strips and then sewing the strips together.

The introduction of the rotary cutter has literally revolutionized the art of quilt making. By using a rotary cutter and acrylic ruler, you can almost eliminate the use of templates that are used for traditional piecing. In addition, the time spent cutting and piecing can be literally cut in half.

You can cut the fabric with a sharp scissors, but you will be able to save time and actually be more accurate by using a rotary cutter.

Start by using the proper tools. You will need a rotary cutter along with its protective mat. Don't try to substitute anything for the mat; it won't work. The mat designed to accompany a rotary cutter is self-healing and it can't dull the cutter blade. There are several brands of cutters currently on the market. They all look a little bit like a pizza cutter with very, very sharp blades. In fact, the blades are so sharp that the cutters are sold with protective guards. This guard should only be removed when you are actually cutting fabric. If you drop your cutter without its guard or cut across a pin, you can dull the blade. A dull blade should be replaced immediately since it will not cut fabric correctly. To keep from hurting yourself as you cut with this extremely sharp instrument, remember one simple rule: **Always cut away from your body.**

In addition to the cutter and its accompanying mat, you will need a straight edge. There are many acrylic rulers currently on the market which are intended for use with the rotary cutter. The rulers usually have markings on the surface which will help in accurate cutting. For most of the cutting in this book, a ruler of about 6" x 24" will be sufficient. These acrylic rulers are printed with grids that are extremely helpful in accurate cutting.

Before you begin to cut your strips, you must make sure that your fabric is perfectly straight. It will be necessary to straighten the fabric along the edge where it was cut off the bolt, as this is seldom cut straight. Fold fabric in half making sure selvages are even, then fold again (**Fig 3**). This means that you will be cutting through four layers at all times. You may want to press down the folds so that your fabric is easier to handle.

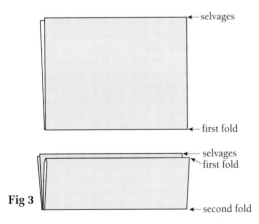

Fig 3

Carefully line up your fold line along one of the horizontal lines of your mat. Place your ruler along the edge of the fabric and cut off the raggedy edge (**Fig 4**). Once you have made this initial cut, you can use this straight edge to align your additional measurements. Place your ruler along the edge that you just straightened, lining up the correct measurement line on your ruler (for your size strip) with the straight edge of the fabric; begin cutting your strips (**Fig 5**).

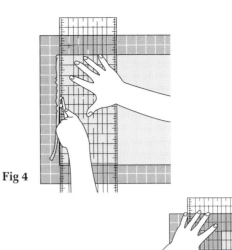

Fig 4

Fig 5

Hint: Make the initial cut (**Fig 4**) with your left hand and the succeeding cuts (**Fig 5**) with your right hand, assuming that you are right handed. The force of the cutter against the mat will compensate for any lack of power you have in your left hand.

Using Templates

Several of the quilts in this collection require triangles for completion. The patterns for these triangles are called "templates" in quilting. The patterns for the necessary templates are given full size and appear on pages 21 to 23.

Note: The template patterns are printed without seam allowance. In quilting the traditional seam allowance is 1/4", and you must allow for these seam allowances when making your templates.

To make templates, lay a piece of tracing paper over the pattern pieces in the book and carefully trace the pattern pieces adding the 1/4" seam allowance all around. (Do not photocopy the pieces instead of tracing. Photocopy machines are not exact, and your pieces may not fit together.) Carefully glue your tracing onto heavy cardboard or plastic. Special plastic for making templates is available in quilt, craft or stationery stores. If you use a clear plastic, you can trace directly onto plastic and eliminate the gluing.

Once you have made your template, carefully cut it out. It is important that your templates be cut out carefully because if they are not accurate, the patchwork will not fit together. Use a pair of good-size sharp scissors (not the same scissors that you use to cut fabric), a single-edged razor blade or a craft knife. Be careful not to bend the corners of the triangles.

Hold your pencil or marker at an angle so that the point is against the side of the template and trace around the template. Continue moving the template and tracing it on fabric the required number of times, moving from left to right and always keeping straight lines parallel with grain.

You can use your rotary cutter to cut several layers at once. Fold fabric so you have as many layers as the number of triangles needed. Lay your template on the wrong side of the fabric which has been folded. Place it so that as many straight sides of the piece as possible are parallel to the crosswise and lengthwise grain of the fabric. Now trace around the template. Then use your acrylic ruler and rotary cutter along the traced lines, making certain that you cut away from your body.

Sewing the Strips

All the quilts in *Quilts in a Hurry* are intended to be sewn on the machine. Machine piecing is done with the straight stitch foot and throat plate on the machine. Set your machine for about 10 stitches to the inch and use a size 14 needle. The traditional seam allowance in quilting is 1/4" so you are going to need some way to make sure that you sew with a perfect 1/4" seam. If your machine has the 1/4" marked on the throat plate you are in luck. If not, measure 1/4" from your needle hole to the right side of the presser foot and place a piece of tape on the plate. Keep the edge of your piece lined up with the tape and you will be able to sew a perfect 1/4" seam.

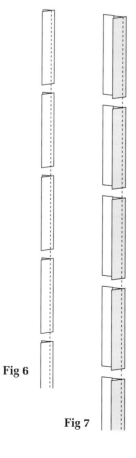

Fig 6

Fig 7

Most of the quilts begin with sewing strips of different colors together. Place the first two fabrics right sides together, matching edges. When you have sewn the first strips together, don't end your thread; just continue feeding the next two strips (**Fig 6**). This is called chain piecing. When you have made a continuous row of strips, snip them apart. Don't worry about threads coming undone. They will eventually be anchored by cross seams.

When you have finished sewing the first two strips, begin chain piecing the next color if it is required and then the next (**Fig 7**). After you have joined all the pieces together, press the seams flat to one side, not open. Generally seams can be pressed in the same direction.

But avoid pressing darker pieces so they fall under light pieces since they may show through when the quilt is completed.

After you have sewn all of the strips, the individual quilt instructions will tell you how to cut the strips into squares and how to join the squares into blocks. Again be sure that you continue to press your seams to one side. You may want to press the seams in opposite directions on alternate rows. This will help to keep seams that are crossed with other seams from bunching at crossing points. You can clip excess fabric at these points if necessary. Just be sure to iron all seams before they are crossed with another seam. When crossing seams be especially careful to match seam to seam.

Hint: As you sew, be careful of fabric's tendency to stretch. This is especially true along bias edges, such as the long sides of triangles. Sewing machines are not infallible. Some constantly fight to stretch the top fabric. You can learn to win. You may be forced to ease the top fabric while stretching the bottom fabric on some seams. It helps if you try to feed the fabric through the machine with the grain straight at all times. Be especially careful of stretching the bias seam allowances. Whenever possible, sew from the large end to the pointed end of a piece, and always iron in the direction of the grain.

Blocking the Blocks

When you have completed a block, it must be "blocked" before it is joined to another block. The term "blocking" means keeping the edges straight on all sides of the quilt so it will be a perfect rectangle when finished. The term applies to the quilt's parts as well as to an entire quilt, so the blocking process is a continuous one from start to finish.

Place the completed block on the ironing board and pull the edges straight with your fingers. Cover the block with a damp cloth and steam with a warm iron (or use a steam iron). Iron the block perfectly flat with no puckers starting with the edges first and the center last. Move the iron as little as possible to keep the block from stretching.

Joining the Blocks

After you have pieced and blocked the required number of blocks for your quilt, lay them out to get the final effect before setting them together.

Using the 1/4" seam allowance, join the blocks in horizontal or vertical rows. When rows are completed, join two rows together, matching seam lines. Then add additional rows.

Hint: When crossing seams, be especially careful to match seam to seam. One learns to do this fairly accurately while sewing by feeling with the fingers. It helps if the lower seam is turned one way and the top seam the other, so press seams for odd numbered rows in one direction; even numbered in the other.

Adding Borders

Although we give measurements for border strips, we recommend that before cutting your border strips, you measure the quilt top and cut your borders to the exact size. If you have made some mistakes in the piecing (for instance, if you made your blocks with a larger than 1/4" seam allowance) this will be the time to adjust your border measurements.

Using the 1/4" seam allowance, attach one side border to the right side of the quilt and one to the left. Then attach the top and bottom borders. Use the 1/4" seam allowance at all times. Repeat for additional borders.

Preparing the Quilt Top

Give the quilt top a final blocking, making sure all corners are square and all seams are pressed to one side.

We have made suggestions for machine quilting your quilt top, but you may wish to follow your own quilting plan. However you are planning to quilt your top, you will need to mark the quilting pattern before joining the top to the batting.

If you prefer to tie your quilt, skip the next section on marking the quilting design.

Marking the Quilting Design

Mark all quilting lines on the **right** side of the fabric. For marking use a hard lead pencil, chalk or other special quilt marking materials. If you quilt right on the marked lines, they will not show. Be sure to test any marking material to find one that works best for you.

A word of caution: Marking lines which are intended to disappear after quilting - either by exposure to air or with water - may become permanent when set with a hot iron. Therefore, don't iron your quilt top after you have marked your quilting pattern.

If you are quilting around shapes, you may not need to mark your line if you feel that you can accurately gauge the quilting line as you work. If you are quilting "in the ditch" of the seam (the space right in the seam), marking is not necessary. Other quilting patterns will need to be marked.

Attaching Batting and Backing

There are a number of different types of batting on the market. Very thin batting will require a great deal of quilting to hold it (quilting lines no more than 1" apart); very thick batting can be used **only** for tied quilts.

For most quilt projects, you are better off with a medium weight bonded polyester sheet batting. There are currently on the market battings recommended for machine quilting. If you are planning to machine quilt, you should investigate these battings.

We have indicated the amount of fabric required for the backing in each pattern. If you prefer another fabric, buy a backing fabric that is soft and loosely woven so that the

quilting needle can pass through easily. Bed sheets are usually not good backing materials.

Since the quilts in this book are wider than fabric width, you will have to sew lengths together to make your quilt backing. Cut off selvages and seam pieces together carefully; iron seam open. **This is the only time in making a quilt that seams should be pressed open.** By seaming several lengths of fabric from the quilt top, an interesting pattern can be created on the back as seen in the photo below.

Cut batting and backing larger than the quilt top: about 2" wider than quilt top on all sides. Place backing, wrong side up, on flat surface. Place batting on top of this, matching outer edges.

Hint: Remove batting from its packaging a day in advance and open it out full size. This will help to get the batting to lie flat.

The layers of the quilt must be held together before quilting. There are two methods for doing this: thread basting and safety pin basting.

For thread basting: First, pin backing and batting together; then baste with long stitches, starting in the center and sewing toward the edges in a number of diagonal lines. Now center quilt top, right side up, on top of the batting. Baste the top to the batting and backing layers in the same manner.

For safety pin basting: This is a new method of preparing a quilt for quilting. Because you don't have to put your hand under the quilt as you do when you are thread basting, the quilt top does not move out of position. Layer the backing, batting and quilt top and pin through all three layers at once. Start pinning from the center and work out to the edges, placing the pins no more than 4" to 6" apart. Think of your quilt plan as you work and make certain that your pins avoid the prospective quilting lines. Choose rustproof pins that are size #1 or #2.

Quilting

Any of the quilts in this collection can be hand quilted. However, if you want to make quilts in a hurry, machine quilting is a necessity. If you have never used a sewing machine for quilting, you might want to read some more about the technique. *Quilting for People Who Don't Have Time to Quilt* by Marti Michell and *A Beginner's Guide to Machine Quilting* by Judi Tyrrell, both published by ASN Publishing, are excellent introductions to machine quilting. These books are available at your local quilt store or department, or write the publisher for a list of sources.

You do not need a special machine for quilting. You can machine quilt with almost any home sewing machine. Just make sure that it is in good working order and that the presser foot is not set for too much pressure which can cause rippling. An even-feed foot is a good investment if you are going to machine quilt since it feeds the top and bottom layers through the machine evenly.

Use fine transparent nylon thread in the top and regular sewing thread in the bobbin.

In order to fit a large quilt under the arm of the sewing machine it will be necessary to fold the quilt so that it is manageable. If you are quilting in horizontal and vertical lines, you will make your first row of quilting along a center seam. Now starting at the sides, roll the quilt to within four to five inches of this center seam. Then, roll the quilt up from the bottom to within a few inches of where you want to begin sewing.

If you are quilting diagonally, your first row of quilting will go from one corner to the opposite corner. You will roll your quilt to within four to five inches of that first diagonal quilting line. Then roll the quilt up from bottom corner to within a few inches of where you will begin sewing.

With the rolled quilt in your lap, place the quilt so that you are in the right position to begin. Lower the presser foot and start. Make certain that you have a table on the other side of the machine to catch the completed work. Otherwise the weight of the quilt can cause a problem. Work from the center out, re-rolling the quilt as you work.

To **quilt-in-the-ditch** of a seam (this is actually stitching in the space between two pieces of fabric that have been sewn together), use your hands to pull the blocks or pieces apart and machine stitch right between the two pieces. Try to keep your stitching just to the side of the seam that does not have the bulk of the seam allowance under it. When you have finished stitching, the quilting will be practically hidden in the seam.

We have used **straight line machine quilting** next to a seam (as in "Star and Stripes") and diagonally through the blocks (as in "Blue Delft Sunshine and Shadow" and "Another Trip Around the World"). You may want to mark these quilting lines with a ruler. It may take a little practice to feel in control and keep the lines of quilting straight.

Free form machine quilting is done with a darning foot and the feed dogs down on your sewing machine. It can be used to quilt around a design or to quilt a motif (as seen in many of the borders including "Ribbons and Ribbons", "Double Zig Zag", and "Southwest Trips"). Mark your quilting design as described in Marking the Quilting Design on page 6. Free form machine quilting takes practice to master because you are controlling the quilt through the machine rather than the machine moving the quilt. With free form machine quilting you can quilt in any direction--up and down, side to side and even in circles without pivoting the quilt around the needle.

Tying the Quilt

Use knitting worsted weight yarn (washable of course), crochet thread, several strands of embroidery floss or other washable material.

Work from the center of the quilt out, adjusting any excess fullness of batting as you go. Thread an 18" length of yarn into a large-eyed needle. Do not knot! Take the needle down from the top through all three layers, leaving about 1" of yarn on the right side. Bring the needle back up from the wrong side to the right side, about 1/8" from where the needle first entered. Tie a firm knot, then cut, leaving both ends about 1/2" long. Make sufficient ties to keep the three layers together.

Attaching the Binding

Place the quilt on a flat surface and carefully trim the backing and batting 1/2" beyond the quilt top edge. Measure the quilt top and cut two 2"-wide binding strips the length of your quilt (for sides). Right sides together, sew one side strip to one side of the quilt with 1/4" seam allowance (seam allowance should be measured from outer edge of quilt top fabric, not outer edge of batting/backing). Turn binding to back and turn under 1/4" on raw edge; slipstitch to backing. Do other side in same manner. For top and bottom edge binding strips, measure carefully adding 1/2" to each end; cut strips 2" wide. To eliminate raw edges at corners, turn the extra 1/2" to wrong side before stitching to top and bottom. Finish in same manner as sides.

Another Trip Around the World

Here is our version of one of the most popular quilts. Try to pick fabric that does not have a directional print, as our instructions have you turning your blocks in many directions.

Size of Quilt Top:
82" x 98"

Finished Size of Block:
8" x 8"

Setting:
This quilt is made in four sections. Each section is set with four 8" blocks across and five 8" blocks down. The four sections are joined with a 2" wide strip. A 2" square of red print fabric is set in the center of the quilt.

Fabric Requirements:

lt print:	3 3/4 yds (includes first border cut crosswise and pieced)
green print:	3 3/4 yds (includes second border and binding cut crosswise and pieced)
floral print:	1 3/4 yds
red print:	1 3/4 yds
backing fabric:	6 yds

Cutting Requirements:
Note: Do not cut borders before measuring pieced quilt top.

twenty	2 1/2" strips (cut crosswise), lt print
twenty	2 1/2" strips (cut crosswise), floral print
twenty	2 1/2" strips (cut crosswise), green print
twenty	2 1/2" strips (cut crosswise), red print
one	2 1/2" x 2 1/2" square, red print
two	4 1/2" x 82 1/2" (for sides of first border), lt print
two	4 1/2" x 76 1/2" (for top and bottom of first border), lt print
two	4 1/2" x 90 1/2" (for sides of second border), green print
two	4 1/2" x 84 1/2" (for top and bottom of second border), green print

Instructions:

1. Sew strips together into four strip pieced fabrics as shown in **Fig 1**. You will need approximately 5 3/4 yds of Strip 2, Strip 3 and Strip 4 and approximately 7 yds of Strip 1.

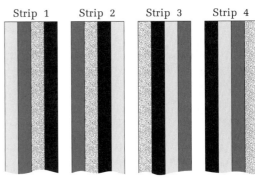

Fig 1

2. Cut strip pieced fabrics crosswise every 2 1/2" (**Fig 2**). You will need 80 pieces from Strip 2, Strip 3 and Strip 4. You will need 98 pieces from Strip 1.

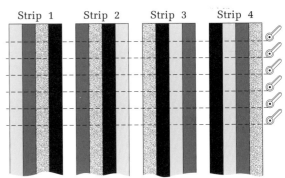

Fig 2

3. Sew pieces together as in **Fig 3** to create block. Make 80 blocks.

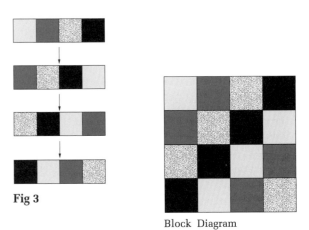

Fig 3

Block Diagram

Color Key

- lt print
- green print
- floral print
- red print

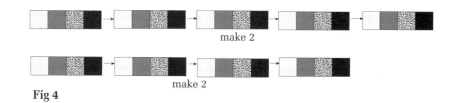

make 2

make 2

Fig 4

4. Sew strips made from Strip1 together to give you two horizontal center strips and two vertical center strips as in **Fig 4**.

5. Refer to **Fig 5** and sew blocks together to make four sections. Sections 1 and 4 are the same; turn remaining blocks a quarter turn then sew together for sections 2 and 3.

(continued)

Fig 5   Sections 1 and 4   Sections 2 and 3

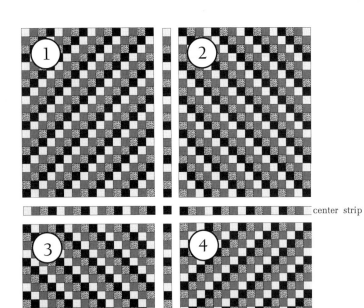

Fig 6

center strip

center strip

6. Following **Fig 6**, join sections 1 and 2 to each side of a vertical center strip; join horizontal center strips to each side of the red square; and then join sections 3 and 4 to each side of remaining vertical center strip.

7. Join the upper and lower sections to each side of center strip as shown in quilt layout.

8. Add the borders, sides first then top and bottom.

9. To finish quilt, follow finishing instructions in *How to Make a Quilt in a Hurry* starting with *Preparing the Quilt Top* on page 6.

Quilting Suggestion:

The photographed quilt was quilted diagonally "around the world" through the red squares.

Quilt Layout

Blue Delft
Sunshine and Shadows

Looking at all the squares in this quilt, it's hard to believe that this is a quilt you can make in a hurry, but this very quilt was cut and pieced in one lazy weekend! If blue is not your color, why not choose shades of another color to make a quilt that is truly your own.

Size of Quilt Top:
80" x 96"

Finished Size of Block:
8" x 8"

Setting:
This quilt is set with eight 8" blocks across and ten 8" blocks down. The quilt is finished with a 4" border of the lt blue print and a 4" border of the medium blue print.

Fabric Requirements:

white print:	1 1/2 yds
lt blue print:	3 yds (includes border cut crosswise and pieced)
med blue print:	3 5/8 yds (includes border and binding cut crosswise and pieced)
dk blue print:	1 1/2 yds
backing fabric:	6 yds

Cutting Requirements:
Note: Do not cut fabric for borders before measuring pieced quilt top.

twenty	2 1/2" strips (cut crosswise), white print
twenty	2 1/2" strips (cut crosswise), lt blue
twenty	2 1/2" strips (cut crosswise), med blue
twenty	2 1/2" strips (cut crosswise), dk blue
two	4 1/12" x 80 1/2" strips (for sides of first border), lt blue print
two	4 1/2" x 64 1/2" strips (for top and bottom of first border), lt blue print
two	4 1/2" x 88 1/2" strips (for sides of second border), med blue print
two	4 1/2" x 80 1/2" strips (for top and bottom of second border), med blue print

Instructions:

1. Sew strips together into four versions as shown in **Fig 1**. Repeat until you have five of each strip pieced fabric. Press seams for A and C in one direction and B and D in the opposite direction to help in matching seams.

Color Key

	1. lt blue
	2. med blue
	3. dk blue
	4. white print

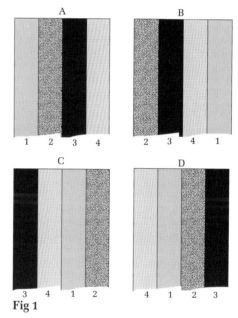

Fig 1

2. Cut strips crosswise every 2 1/2" (**Fig 2**). You will need 80 strips of each strip pieced fabric.

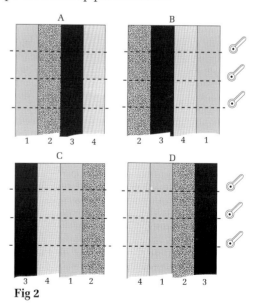

Fig 2

11

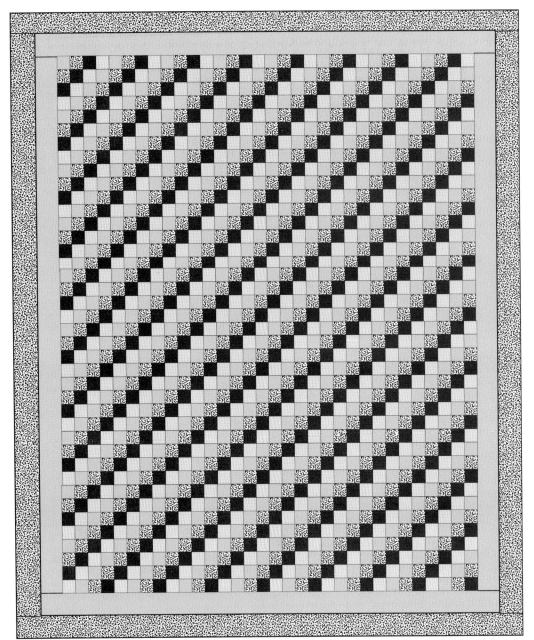

Quilt Layout

Color Key

	1. lt blue
	2. med blue
	3. dk blue
	4. white print

3. Sew strips together as in **Fig 3** to create block. Make 80 blocks.

4. Join the blocks together in ten rows of eight blocks. Join the rows.

5. Add the borders, sides first then top and bottom.

6. To finish quilt, follow finishing instructions in *How to Make a Quilt in a Hurry* starting with *Preparing the Quilt Top* on page 6.

Quilting Suggestion:

The photographed quilt was quilted in diagonal rows through the lt blue and dk blue squares.

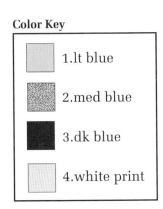

Fig 3

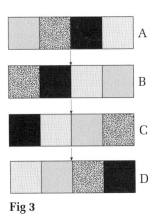

Block Diagram

12

Blue Pinwheels

This is a traditional pattern that is made in a hurry with our quick-to-piece instructions. What makes this quilt so interesting is the use of many blue prints and many light prints to create the pinwheels.

Size of Quilt Top:
86" x 102"

Finished Size of Block:
12" x 12"

Setting:
The blocks are set in eight diagonal rows. Fourteen half blocks are used to finish the sides with four quarter blocks at each corner. The quilt is finished with two 4" borders.

Fabric Requirements:

blue prints:	5 1/4 yds (includes border and binding cut crosswise and pieced)
lt prints:	4 1/2 yds (includes border cut crosswise and pieced)
backing fabric:	6 yds

Template Requirements (page 21):
Template C

Cutting Requirements:
Note: Do not cut fabric for borders before measuring pieced quilt top.

twelve	15" x 22" rectangles of blue print (These may all be cut from the same blue fabric or from assorted blues as in the photographed quilt.)
twelve	15" x 22" rectangles of lt prints (These may be cut from the same light fabric or from assorted fabrics as in the photographed quilt.)
eighteen	Template C triangles, blue print
eighteen	Template C triangles, lt print
two	4 1/2" x 86 1/2" strips (for first side borders), lt print
two	4 1/2" x 78 1/2" strips (for first top and bottom borders), lt print
two	4 1/2" x 94 1/2" strips (for second side borders), blue print
two	4 1/2" x 86 1/2" strips (for second top and bottom borders), blue print

Instructions:

1. Starting at least 1/2" from all edges of WRONG side of lighter pieces, draw a grid with lines 6 7/8" apart, being sure that squares are drawn ACCURATELY. You will have a grid with two squares down and three across (**Fig 1**).

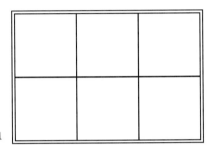

Fig 1

2. Draw diagonal lines through every other square (**Fig 2**).

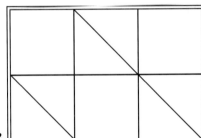

Fig 2

3. Then draw diagonal lines through all the empty squares in the opposite direction (**Fig 3**).

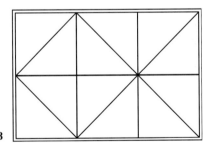

Fig 3

4. Place marked fabric right sides together with dark fabric. Press together lightly and pin or baste the two pieces to hold in place. Referring to **Fig 4** and starting in a corner where the diagonal line goes from the outside to the inside, stitch 1/4" to the left of the drawn diagonal line. Continue stitching along the diagonal lines until you reach the corner where you started. Make sure you have stitched on both sides of all diagonal lines.

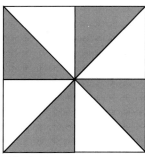

Block Diagram

Color Key

blue

white

5. Remove pins or basting and press well. Using scissors or rotary cutter and mat, cut along every marked line— horizontal, vertical and diagonal. Press each pieced square open with the seam allowance toward the darker side. Trim "dog ears" from each square, **Fig 5**.

6. Sew four pieced squares together to form Pinwheel Block as in Block Diagram. Repeat with remaining pieced squares until you have 32 blocks.

7. Sew light print and blue print triangles from Template C to pieced squares to create the fourteen Half Blocks as in **Fig 6**.

8. Sew light print and blue print triangles from Template C to make the four Quarter Blocks as in **Fig 7**.

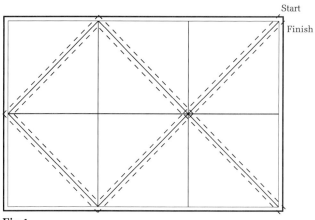

Start

Finish

Fig 4

Fig 6

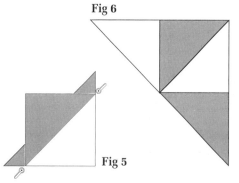

Fig 5

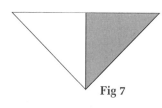

Fig 7

9. The quilt is constructed in diagonal rows. Follow **Fig 8** to make rows, adding Half Blocks or Quarter Blocks at the ends of the rows; then join rows to complete quilt top.

10. Turn the quilt so that the blocks are on point as in the quilt layout.

11. Add the light borders to sides and then to top and bottom. Add dark borders to sides and then to top and bottom.

12. To finish quilt, follow finishing instructions in *How to Make a Quilt in a Hurry* starting with *Preparing the Quilt Top* on page 6.

Quilting Suggestion:

The photographed quilt was quilted in the ditch around the triangles.

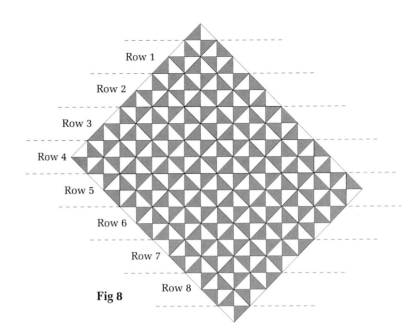

Fig 8

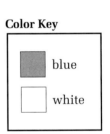

Color Key

blue

white

Quilt Layout

16

If the Irish Were Amish

Who said that an Irish Chain always had to be green and white? Why not make an Irish chain in Amish colors? If Amish colors are not to your liking, use these instructions to make an Irish Chain in colors of your choice. This is a quilt that really can be made in a hurry; cut and piece it over a weekend. Your friends and relatives will be amazed.

Size of Quilt Top:
86" x 106"

Finished Size of Block:
10" x 10"

Setting:
This quilt is made with two blocks, Block A and Block B. The quilt is made with four A Blocks and four B Blocks set across and five A Blocks and five B Blocks down. The quilt is finished with a 3" border of the fuchsia fabric.

Fabric Requirements:

black: 4 1/4 yds
blue: 1 3/4 yds
fuchsia: 4 yds (includes border and binding cut crosswise and pieced)
backing fabric: 6 yds

Cutting Requirements:

Note: Do not cut fabric for borders before measuring pieced quilt top.

twenty-five	2 1/2" strips (cut crosswise), black
twenty-three	2 1/2" strips (cut crosswise), blue
thirty-seven	2 1/2" strips (cut crosswise), fuchsia
twelve	6 1/2" strips (cut crosswise), black
two	3 1/2" x 100 1/2" strips (for side borders), fuchsia
two	3 1/2" x 86 1/2" strips (for top and bottom borders), fuchsia

Block A Diagram   Block B Diagram

Instructions:

BLOCK A
1. Sew black, fuchsia and blue 2 1/2" strips together into three versions as shown in **Fig 1**. You will need approximately 5 3/4 yds of Strips 1 and 2 and 3 yds of Strip 3.

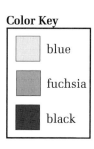

Color Key

	blue
	fuchsia
	black

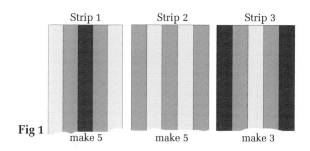

Fig 1
make 5   make 5   make 3

2. Cut strips crosswise every 2 1/2" until you have 80 strips from Strip 1 and 2 and 40 strips from Strip 3 (**Fig 2**).

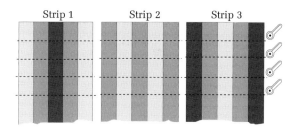

Strip 1   Strip 2   Strip 3

Fig 2

3. Sew strips together as in **Fig 3**. Make 40 Block A.

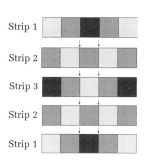

Strip 1
Strip 2
Strip 3
Strip 2
Fig 3   Strip 1

BLOCK B

1. Sew two fuchsia 2 1/2" strips on either side of black 6 1/2" strip (**Fig 4**). You will need approximately 5 1/2 yds of Strip 4.

2. Cut strips crosswise every 2 1/2" (**Fig 5**) until you have 80 strips.

3. Sew two black 2 1/2" strips to either side of black 6 1/2" strip (**Fig 6**). You will need approximately 7 1/2 yds of Strip 5.

4. Cut strips crosswise every 6 1/2" until you have 40 strips (**Fig 7**).

5. Sew strips together as in **Fig 8** until you have 40 Block B.

Strip 4

Fig 4

Fig 5

Strip 5

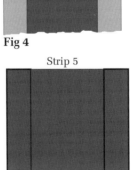

Fig 6

Fig 7

18

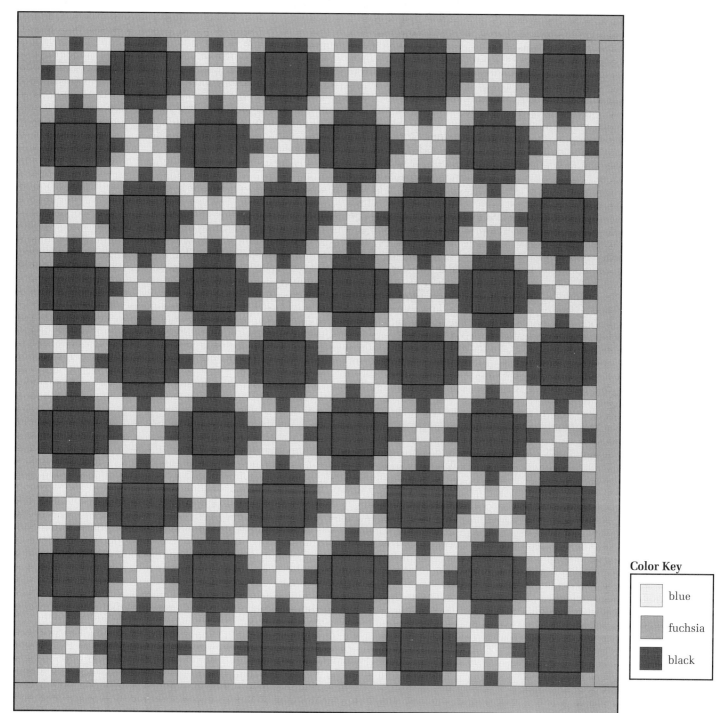

Quilt Layout

Color Key

☐	blue
▓	fuchsia
■	black

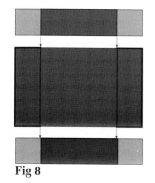

Fig 8

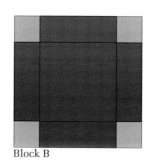

Block B

JOINING BLOCKS

1. Join blocks following quilt layout.

2. Add fuchsia borders to sides and then to top and bottom.

3. To finish quilt, follow finishing instructions in *How to Make a Quilt in a Hurry* starting with *Preparing the Quilt Top* on page 6.

(continued)

Quilting Suggestion:

The photographed quilt was quilted in diagonal lines as shown in **Fig 9**. The Quilting Template on page 22 was used to mark the borders. Do not add seam allowance when making Quilting Template.

Fig 9

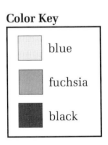

Color Key

	blue
	fuchsia
	black

20

Templates

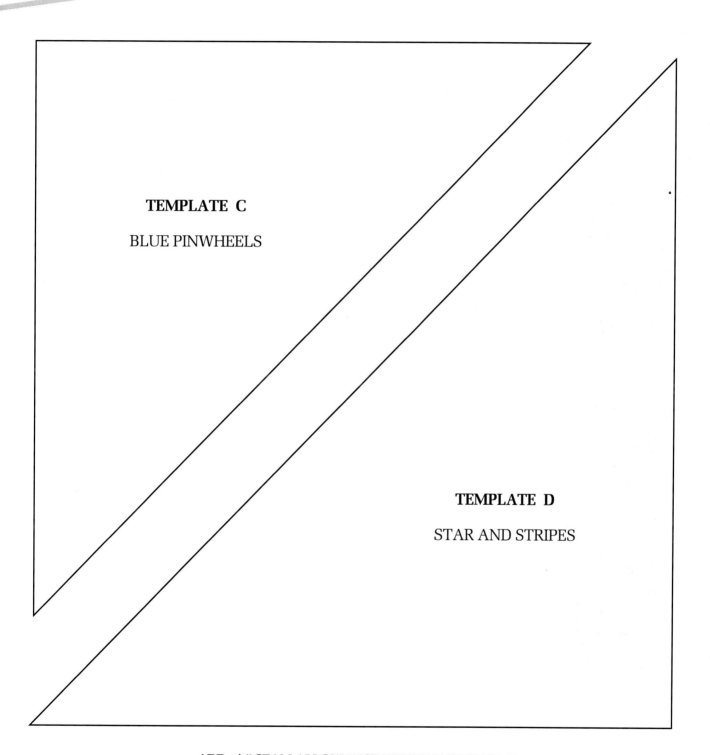

TEMPLATE C

BLUE PINWHEELS

TEMPLATE D

STAR AND STRIPES

ADD 1/4" SEAM ALLOWANCE WHEN MAKING TEMPLATES

QUILTING TEMPLATE

Do not add seam allowance.

**ADD 1/4" SEAM ALLOWANCE
WHEN MAKING TEMPLATES**

TEMPLATE A

NINE PATCH JEWELS

RIBBONS & RIBBONS

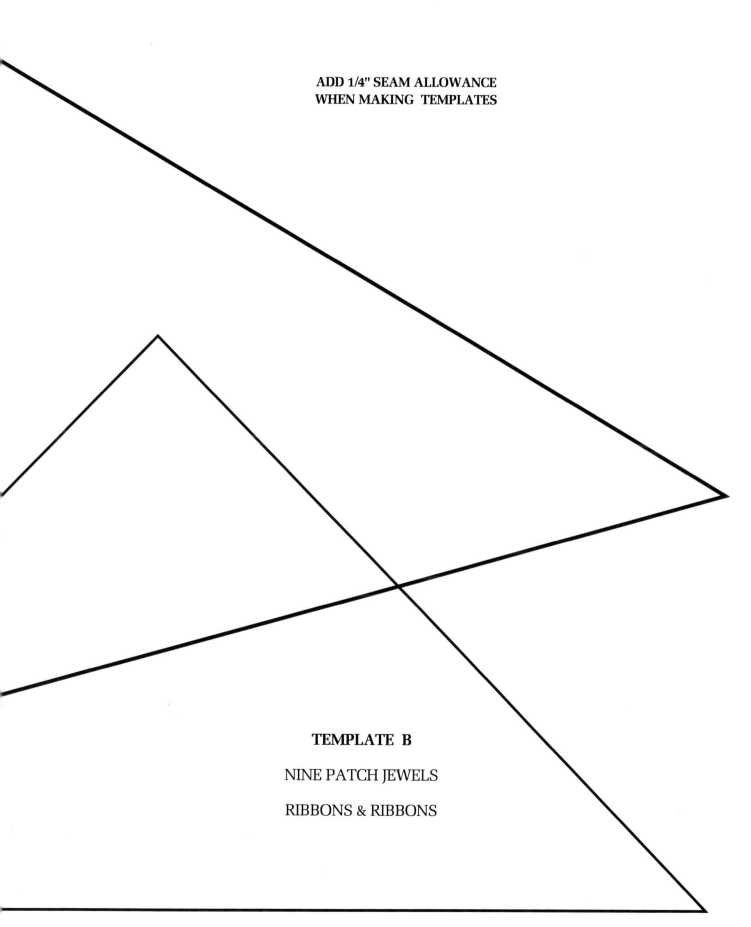

ADD 1/4" SEAM ALLOWANCE
WHEN MAKING TEMPLATES

TEMPLATE B

NINE PATCH JEWELS

RIBBONS & RIBBONS

Nine Patch Jewels

This very simple quilt is enhanced by the choice of colors for the blocks. We started with the black print, which reminded us of jewels and then chose our accent colors to match.

Size of Quilt Top:
87 1/2" x 105"

Finished Size of Block:
12" x 12"

Setting:
This quilt is made with two blocks, Block A and Block B, that alternate in ten diagonal rows. Triangles cut with Templates A and B are used to fill out the edges and corners.

Fabric Requirements:

red print: 2 yds
blue print: 5/8 yd
gold print: 3 1/4 yd
black print: 4 yds (includes binding cut crosswise and pieced)
backing fabric: 6 yds

Template Requirements (pages 22 and 23):

Template A
Template B

Cutting Requirements:

fifteen	4 1/2" strips (cut crosswise), red print
four	4 1/2" strips (cut crosswise), blue print
thirteen	4 1/2" strips (cut crosswise), black print
twenty-five	4 1/2" strips (cut crosswise), gold print
eighteen	Template A triangles, black print
four	Template B triangles, black print

Block A Diagram

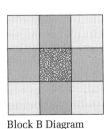

Block B Diagram

Instructions:

BLOCK A

1. Sew black and gold 4 1/2" strips together into two versions as shown in **Fig 1**. You will need approximately 3 yds of Strip 1 and 6 yds of Strip 2.

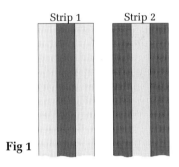

Fig 1

2. Cut strips crosswise every 4 1/2" (**Fig 2**). You will need 20 strips of Strip 1 and 40 strips of Strip 2.

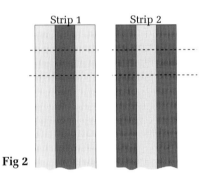

Fig 2

3. Sew strips together as in **Fig 3**. Make 20 Block A.

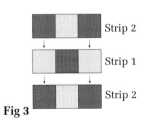

Fig 3

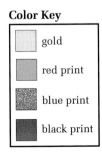

Color Key

	gold
	red print
	blue print
	black print

(continued on page 26)

BLOCK B

1. Sew two gold 4 1/2" strips on either side of red 4 1/2" strip, and two red 4 1/2" strips on either side of blue 4 1/2" strip (**Fig 4**). You will need approximately 8 1/2 yds of Strip 3 and 4 1/4 yds of Strip 4.

2. Cut strips crosswise every 4 1/2" (**Fig 5**). You will need 30 strips of Strip 4 and 60 strips of Strip 3.

3. Sew strips together as in **Fig 6** until you have 30 Block B.

JOINING BLOCKS

1. The quilt is constructed in diagonal rows. Follow the diagram in **Fig 7** adding Template A and B triangles at the ends of the rows; then join rows to complete quilt top.

2. Turn the quilt so that the blocks are on point as in the quilt layout.

3. To finish quilt, follow finishing instructions in *How to Make a Quilt in a Hurry* starting with *Preparing the Quilt Top* on page 6.

Quilting Suggestion:

The photographed quilt was quilted in the ditch around each square.

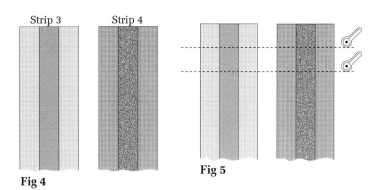

Strip 3   Strip 4

Fig 4

Fig 5

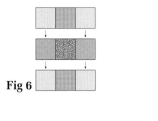

Fig 6

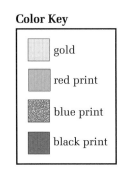

Color Key

gold

red print

blue print

black print

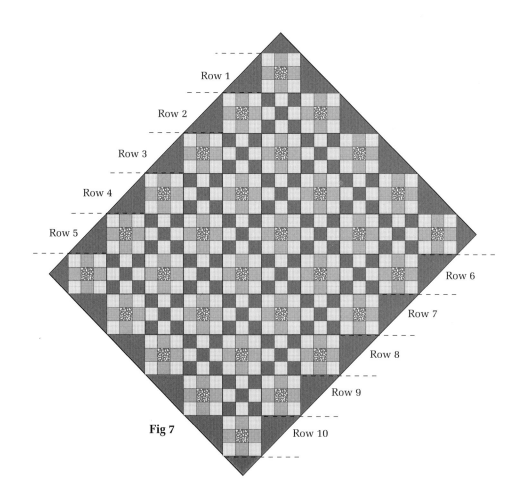

Row 1
Row 2
Row 3
Row 4
Row 5
Row 6
Row 7
Row 8
Row 9
Row 10

Fig 7

Quilt Layout

Nine-Patch Flower Garden

If you have ever wondered what to do with fabric with pre-printed blocks — called "cheater blocks"— why not plant a flower garden. If the blocks have sailboats on them, you could have a Nine-Patch Ocean. Just use the same instructions and let your fabric determine your quilt title.

Size of Quilt Top:
83 1/2" x 109"

Finished Size of Floral Block:
9" x 9"

Finished Size of Nine-Patch Block:
3 3/4" x 3 3/4"

Setting:
The floral blocks are set five across and seven down with sashing created from strips of the gold print and the mauve plus the nine patch blocks. The quilt is finished with borders of both the gold print and mauve.

Fabric Requirements:

gold print: 3 1/2 yds
(includes border cut crosswise and pieced)
mauve: 5 yds (includes border and binding
cut crosswise and pieced)
floral block
fabric: 4 yds*
backing: 6 1/2 yds
*Fabric Note: Check the fabric to make sure that you will have enough printed fabric for the 35 blocks.

Cutting Requirements:
Note: Do not cut fabric borders before measuring pieced quilt top.

thirty-five	9 1/2" x 9 1/2" floral squares
thirty-one	1 3/4" strips (cut crosswise), gold print
fifty	1 3/4" strips (cut crosswise), mauve
two	4 1/2" x 93 1/2" strips (for first side border), gold print,
two	4 1/2" x 76" strips (for first top and bottom border), gold print
two	4 1/2" x 101 1/2" strips (for second side border), mauve
two	4 1/2" x 84" strips (for second top and bottom border), mauve

Instructions:

1. For sashing strips, join 2 mauve strips to a gold strip (**Fig 1**). Repeat for a total of 21 pieced strips. Cut crosswise every 9 1/2" until you have 82 pieces (**Fig 2**).

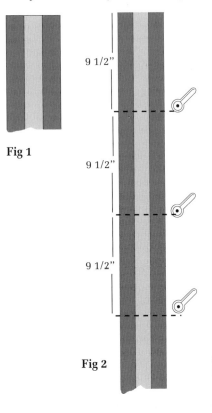

9 1/2"

Fig 1

9 1/2"

9 1/2"

Fig 2

Color Key

	mauve
	gold print

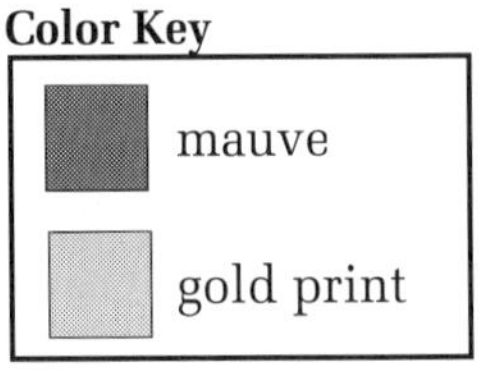

2. For Nine-Patch blocks, sew 2 mauve strips to a gold strip to create pieced Strip A. Repeat for a total of 2 pieced Strip A. Then sew 2 gold strips to one mauve strip to create pieced Strip B (**Fig 3**). Repeat for a total of 4 pieced Strip B. Cut crosswise every 1 3/4" (**Fig 4**) until you have 48 pieces of Strip A and 96 pieces of Strip B. Sew a Strip B piece on each side of a Strip A piece (**Fig 5**) until you have 48 Nine-Patch blocks.

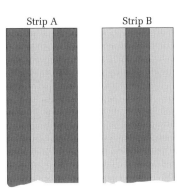

Strip A   Strip B

Fig 3

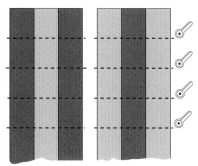

Fig 4

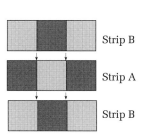

Strip B

Strip A

Strip B

Fig 5

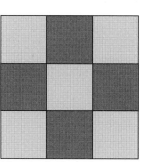

Nine Patch Block Diagram

(continued)

3. For long sashing strips, join 8 Nine-Patch blocks to 7 sashing strips (**Fig 6**). Repeat for five more strips.

4. Join 7 floral blocks to 8 sashing strips as shown in **Fig 7**. You now have a vertical strip of 7 joined blocks. Make four more vertical strips.

5. Following quilt layout, join the vertical strips to the long sashing strips created in step 3 above.

6. Add gold print border to sides and then to top and bottom. Add mauve border to sides and then to top and bottom.

7. To finish quilt, follow finishing instructions in *How to Make a Quilt in a Hurry* starting with *Preparing the Quilt Top* on page 6.

Quilting Suggestion:

The photographed quilt was quilted in the ditch around the mauve strips and squares. The Quilting Template on page 22 was used to mark the border. Do not add seam allowance when making Quilting Template.

Fig 6   Fig 7

Quilt Layout

Ribbons and Ribbons

Our traditional Basketweave Quilt takes on a new dimension when the blocks are turned on point. Can you see the "rows of ribbons" threaded through the quilt? This quilt looks difficult and complicated, but it's really quite easy if you follow our instructions.

Size of Quilt Top:
87 1/2" x 105"

Finished Size of Block:
12" x 12"

Setting:
The blocks are set in ten rows diagonally. Triangles made from the Templates A and B are used to fill out the edges and corners.

Fabric Requirements:

Peach print: 2 3/4 yds
Lt print: 2 3/4 yds
Dk green print: 4 3/4 yds (includes binding cut cross wise and pieced)
Backing fabric: 6 yds

Template Requirements (pages 22 and 23):

Template A
Template B

Cutting Requirements:

thirty-four	2 1/2" strips (cut crosswise), peach
thirty-four	2 1/2" strips (cut crosswise), dk green
thirty-four	2 1/2" strips (cut crosswise), lt print
eighteen	Template A triangles, dk green
four	Template B triangles, dk green

Color Key

Instructions:

1. Sew peach, dk green and lt print 2 1/2" strips together as in **Fig 1**.

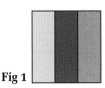

Fig 1

2. Cut strips crosswise every 6 1/2" (**Fig 2**) to make Quarter Blocks. You will need 200 Quarter Blocks.

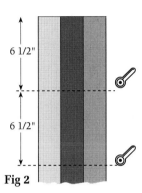

Fig 2

3. Sew Quarter Blocks together as in **Fig 3** noting position of each block. Make 50 Blocks.

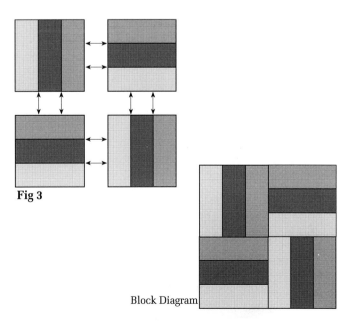

Fig 3

Block Diagram

(continued)

4. The quilt is constructed in diagonal rows. Follow **Fig 4** to make rows, adding triangles made from Templates A and B at ends of the rows.

5. Join rows to create quilt. Turn quilt so that the blocks are on point as in quilt layout.

6. To finish quilt, follow instructions in *How to Make a Quilt in a Hurry*, starting with *Preparing the Quilt Top* on page 6.

Quilting Suggestion:

The photographed quilt was quilted in the ditch along the peach zigzag.

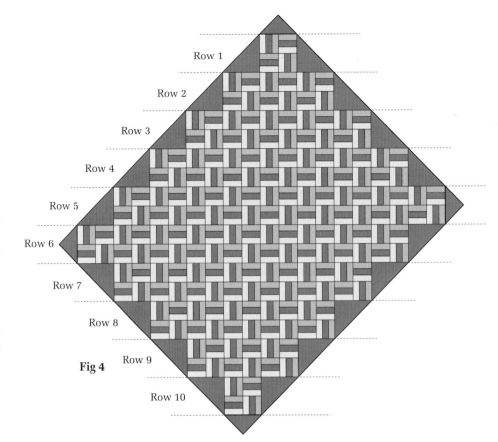

Row 1
Row 2
Row 3
Row 4
Row 5
Row 6
Row 7
Row 8
Row 9
Fig 4
Row 10

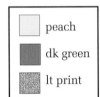

peach
dk green
lt print

Quilt Layout

32

Southwest Trips

The traditional Trip Around the World, enlarged into many "trips" and pieced in Southwest colors, becomes this magnificent Southwest Trips. It is easy to piece, but as with all journeys, you must follow the road map--in this case the quilt layout--or you'll be hopelessly lost.

Size of Quilt Top:
94" x 106"

Finished Size of Block:
12" x 12"

Setting:
This quilt is made with nine small Trip Around the World units with half units filling in where necessary.

Fabric Requirements:

black print:	2 1/4 yds (includes borders cut crosswise and pieced)
dk turquoise print:	3 1/4 yds (includes borders and binding cut crosswise and pieced)
dk rust print:	1 yd
gray print:	1 1/4 yds
lt turquoise print:	1 1/2 yds
lt rust print:	3 yds
med tan print:	1 yd
lt tan print:	3/4 yd
backing fabric:	7 1/2 yds

Color Key

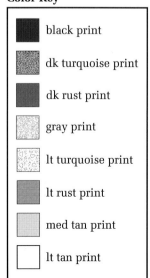

black print

dk turquoise print

dk rust print

gray print

lt turquoise print

lt rust print

med tan print

lt tan print

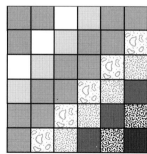

Block Diagram

Cutting Requirements:

Note: Do not cut borders before measuring pieced quilt top.

nine	2 1/2" strips (cut crosswise), black print
nine	2 1/2" strips (cut crosswise), dk turquoise print
twelve	2 1/2" strips (cut crosswise), dk rust print
fifteen	2 1/2" strips (cut crosswise), gray print
nine	2 1/2" x 2 1/2" squares, gray print
eighteen	2 1/2" strips (cut crosswise), lt turquoise print
forty-two	2 1/2" strips (cut crosswise), lt rust print
twelve	2 1/2" strips (cut crosswise), med tan print
nine	2 1/2" strips (cut crosswise), lt tan print
two	4 1/2" x 90 1/2" strips (for sides of first border), black print
two	4 1/2" x 86 1/2" strips (for top and bottom of first border), black print
two	4 1/2" x 98 1/2" strips (for sides of second border), dk turquoise print
two	4 1/2" x 94 1/2" strips (for top and bottom of second border), dk turquoise print

Instructions:

1. Sew strips together into six strip pieced fabrics as shown in **Fig 1**.

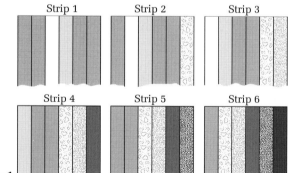

Fig 1

2. Cut strip pieced fabrics crosswise every 2 1/2" (**Fig 2**). You will need 42 of each strip.

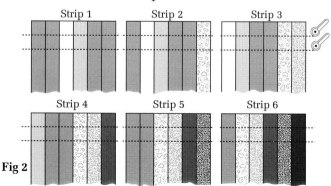

Fig 2

34

3. Sew strips together as in **Fig 3** to create block. Make 42 blocks.

4. To create center strips, sew strips together into strip pieced fabric as shown in **Fig 4**. Cut pieced fabric crosswise every 2 1/2" (**Fig 5**). You will need 39 strips.

5. Sew two blocks (from step 3) to each side of a center strip as in **Fig 6**, being sure to turn one block a quarter turn. Repeat with two more blocks and another center strip.

6. Sew two center strips made in step 4 on each side of the 2 1/2" x 2 1/2" gray print square (**Fig 7**).

Fig 3

Fig 4   **Fig 5**

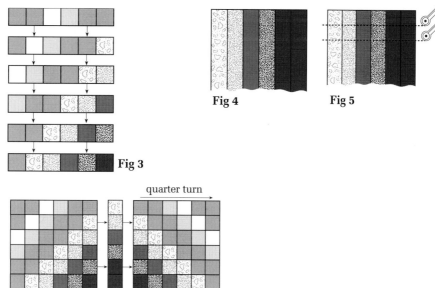

quarter turn

Fig 6

Fig 7

35

7. Sew the three sections made in steps 5 and 6 together to complete the Trip Unit (**Fig 8**).

8. Repeat steps 5 to 7 to complete nine Trip Units.

9. Sew remaining blocks to remaining center strips to form three half units (**Fig 9**).

10. Join three Trip Units and a half unit (**Fig 10**). Repeat two more times.

11. Join the three sections, **Fig 11**, reversing the middle section.

12. Add the borders, sides first, then top and bottom.

13. To finish quilt, follow instructions in *How to Make a Quilt in a Hurry* starting with *Preparing the Quilt Top* on page 6.

Quilting Suggestion:

The photographed quilt was quilted diagonally in the lt and dk turquoise squares and diagonally in the lt and med tan squares. The Quilting Template on page 22 was used to mark the pattern in the borders. Do not add seam allowance when making Quilting Template.

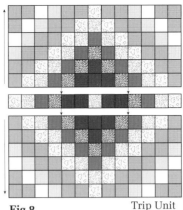

Fig 8   Trip Unit

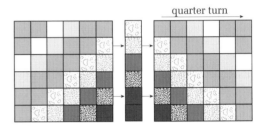

Fig 9

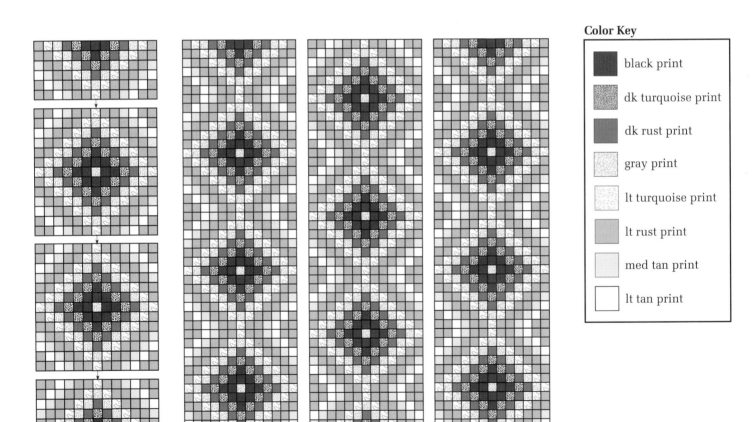

Fig 10

Fig 11

Color Key

■	black print
▨	dk turquoise print
▨	dk rust print
▨	gray print
▨	lt turquoise print
▨	lt rust print
▨	med tan print
□	lt tan print

quarter turn

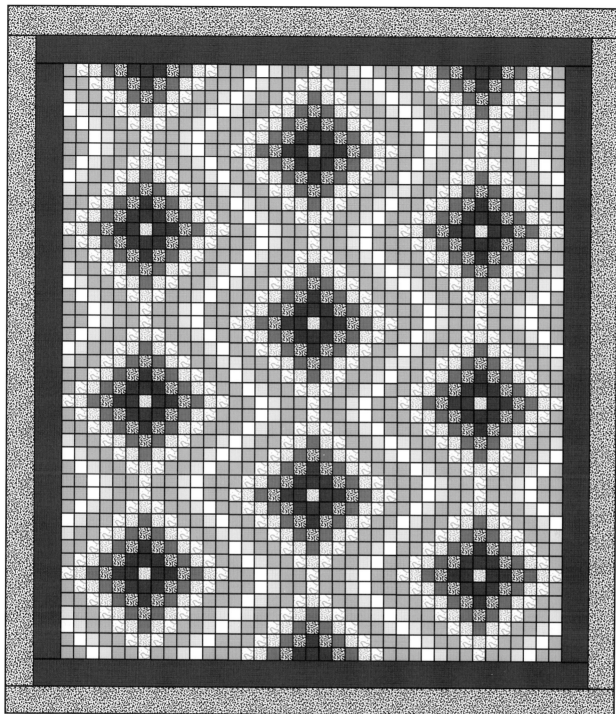

Quilt Layout

Double Zig Zag

A Fence Rail quilt becomes a double zig zag when you use a combination of light and dark fabrics. This is truly a quilt that can be made in a hurry.

Size of Quilt Top:
80" x 104"

Finished Size of Block:
12" x 12"

Setting:
The blocks are set six across and eight down with a 4" border.

Fabric Requirements:

med peach print:	1 3/4 yds
dk peach print:	1 3/4 yds
black print:	1 3/4 yds
lt peach print:	4 yds (includes border)
backing fabric:	6 yds

Cutting Requirements:

Note: Do not cut borders before measuring pieced quilt top.

sixteen	3 1/2" strips (cut crosswise) of each of 4 fabrics
two	4 1/2" x 72 1/2" strips (for side borders), lt peach
two	4 1/2" x 80 1/2" strips (for top and bottom borders), lt peach

Instructions:

1. Sew strips together as shown in **Fig 1**. Repeat with remaining strips until you have 16 pieced strips.

2. Cut strips crosswise every 12 1/2" (**Fig 2**) until you have 48 blocks.

Fig 1

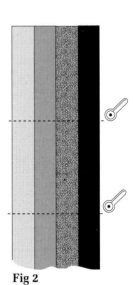

Fig 2

Color Key

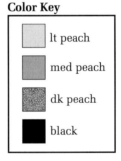

lt peach

med peach

dk peach

black

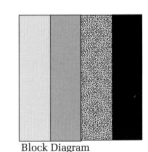

Block Diagram

3. Join blocks, following quilt layout.

4. Add lt peach borders to sides and then to top and bottom.

5. To finish quilt, follow finishing instructions in *How to Make a Quilt in a Hurry*, starting with *Preparing the Quilt Top* on page 6.

Quilting Suggestions:

The quilt shown in the photograph was quilted in the ditch around the black strips. The Quilting Template on page 22 was used to mark the borders.

Quilt Layout

39

Star and Stripes

Start with five strips of fabric; join them; cut them; rearrange them, and lo and behold a center star surrounded by squares of color set on point. While this is a fast quilt to make, don't be in too much of a hurry to join your strips. You have to be extremely accurate in order to have the quilt fit together properly. If you find that you did not sew your strips with a perfect 1/4" seam allowance, you may have to redraft the triangle template.

Size of Quilt Top:
72" x 86"

Finished Size of Block:
7" x 7"

Setting:
This quilt is set with eight 7" blocks across and ten 7" blocks down. The quilt is finished with a 4" border of the lt red fabric and a 4" border of the dark blue fabric.

Fabric Requirements:

med blue print: 3/4 yd
lt blue print: 3/4 yd
dk red print: 3/4 yd
dk blue print: 3 yds (includes border and binding cut crosswise and pieced)
lt red print: 1 3/4 yds (includes border cut crosswise and pieced)
white print: 3 yds
backing fabric: 6 yds

Template Requirements (page 21):

Template D

Cutting Requirements:

Note: Do not cut fabric for borders before measuring pieced quilt top.

thirteen	1 1/2" wide strips (cut crosswise), dk blue print
thirteen	1 1/2" wide strips (cut crosswise), med blue print
thirteen	1 1/2 wide strips (cut crosswise), lt blue print
thirteen	1 1/2" wide strips (cut crosswise), dk red print
thirteen	1 1/2" wide strips (cut crosswise), lt red print
sixty-eight	Template D triangles, white print
twelve	7 1/2" squares, white print
two	4 1/2" x 70 1/2" strips (for sides of first border), lt red print
two	4 1/2" x 64 1/2" strips (for top and bottom of first border, lt red print
two	4 1/2" x 78 1/2" strips (for sides of second border), dk blue print
two	4 1/2" x 72 1/2" strips (for top and bottom of second border), dk blue print

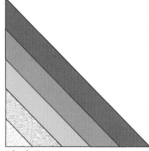

Block Diagram A   Block Diagram B

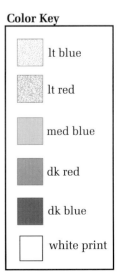

Color Key

	lt blue
	lt red
	med blue
	dk red
	dk blue
	white print

Instructions:

1. Sew strips together in the order shown in **Fig 1**, starting each strip 1" down from previous strip.

2. Repeat until you have 13 strip pieced fabrics.

3. Take Template D (which was used to cut your white triangles) and place it over a strip pieced fabric made in steps 1 and 2 above. As explained in *Using Templates* on page 4, draw around the template as shown in **Fig 2**.

4. Using your rotary cutter and ruler (or a sharp scissors) carefully cut out the triangles. When you are finished, half of your triangles will have lt blue tips (**Fig 3A**) and half will have dk blue tips (**Fig 3B**).

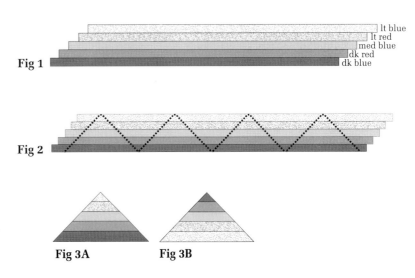

Fig 1 — lt blue / lt red / med blue / dk red / dk blue

Fig 2

Fig 3A   Fig 3B

(continued)

5. Sew a white print triangle to each pieced triangle to form Blocks A and B. The piecing can be done by the chain piecing method as explained in *Sewing the Strips* on page 5.

6. Join the blocks referring to the layout for placement.

7. Add the first border, sides first, then top and bottom. Repeat for second border.

Hint: Be especially careful as you work with the pieced triangles. They have all been cut on the bias and they may have a tendency to stretch with too much handling.

8. To finish quilt, follow finishing instructions in *How to Make a Quilt in a Hurry*, starting with *Preparing the Quilt Top* on page 6.

Quilting Suggestion:

The photographed quilt was quilted in the ditch and around the shapes as shown in **Fig 4**, which illustrates one corner of the quilt. The Quilting Template on page 22 was used to mark the borders. Do not add seam allowance when making Quilting Template.

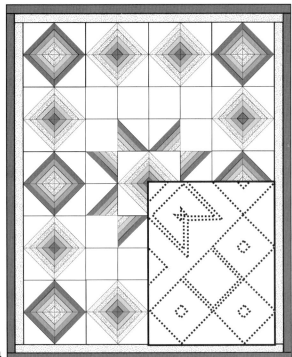

Fig 4

Quilt Layout

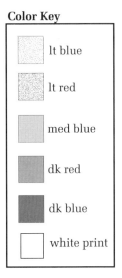

Color Key

	lt blue
	lt red
	med blue
	dk red
	dk blue
	white print

42

▶ Southwest Trips

▲ Double ZigZag

43

◀ Nine-Patch
Flower Garden

▼ Blue Delft
Sunshine and Shadow